Prepare yourself reader!

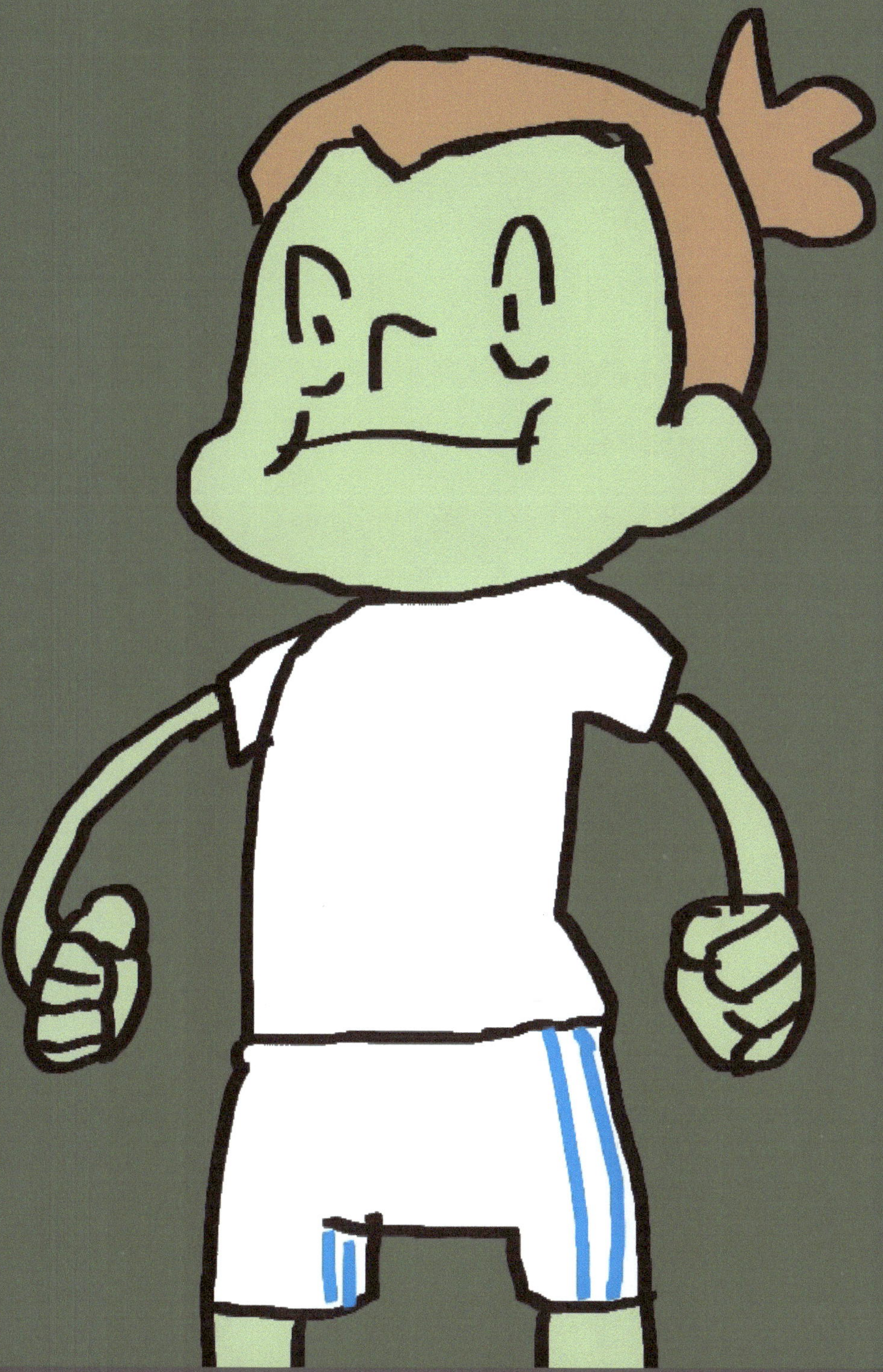

HI ! I'm a digital artist in the US, I
Mostly do digital paintings and some
graphic design here and there.

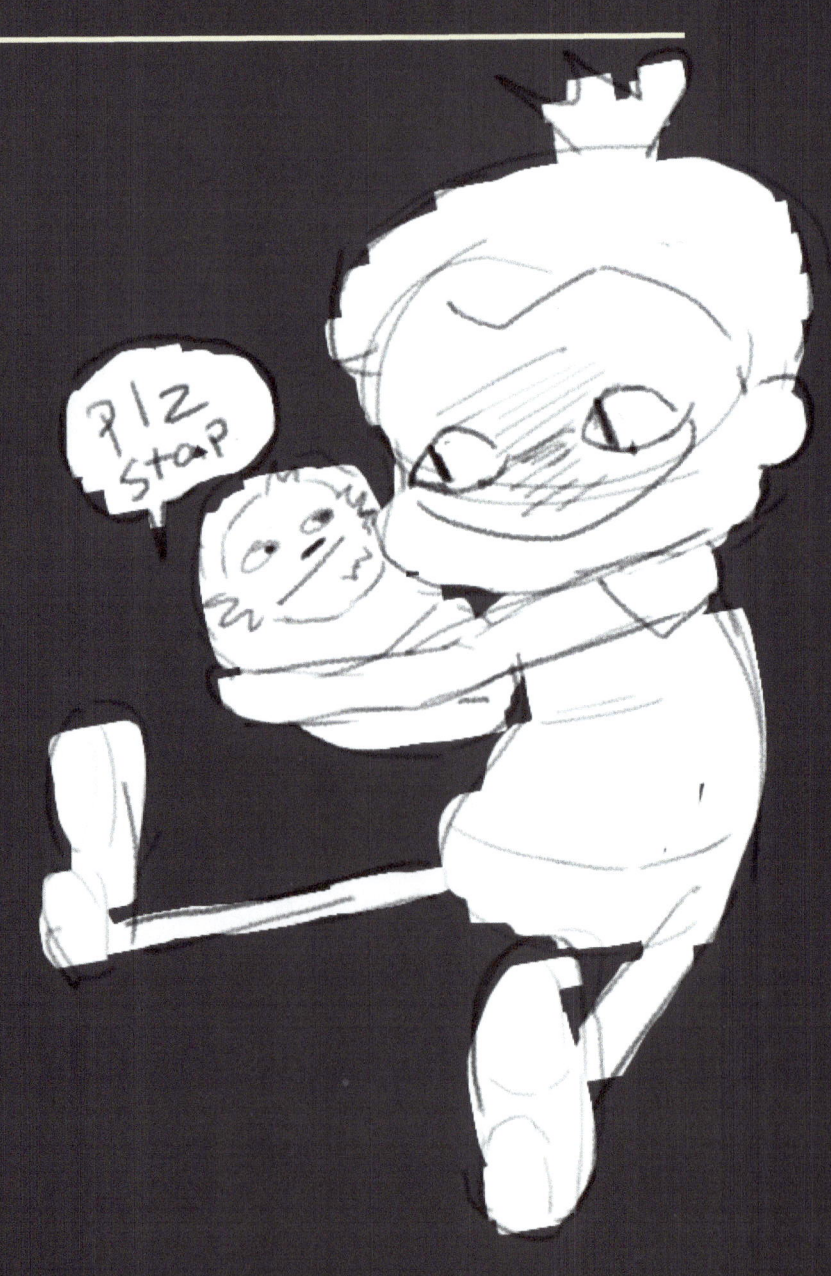

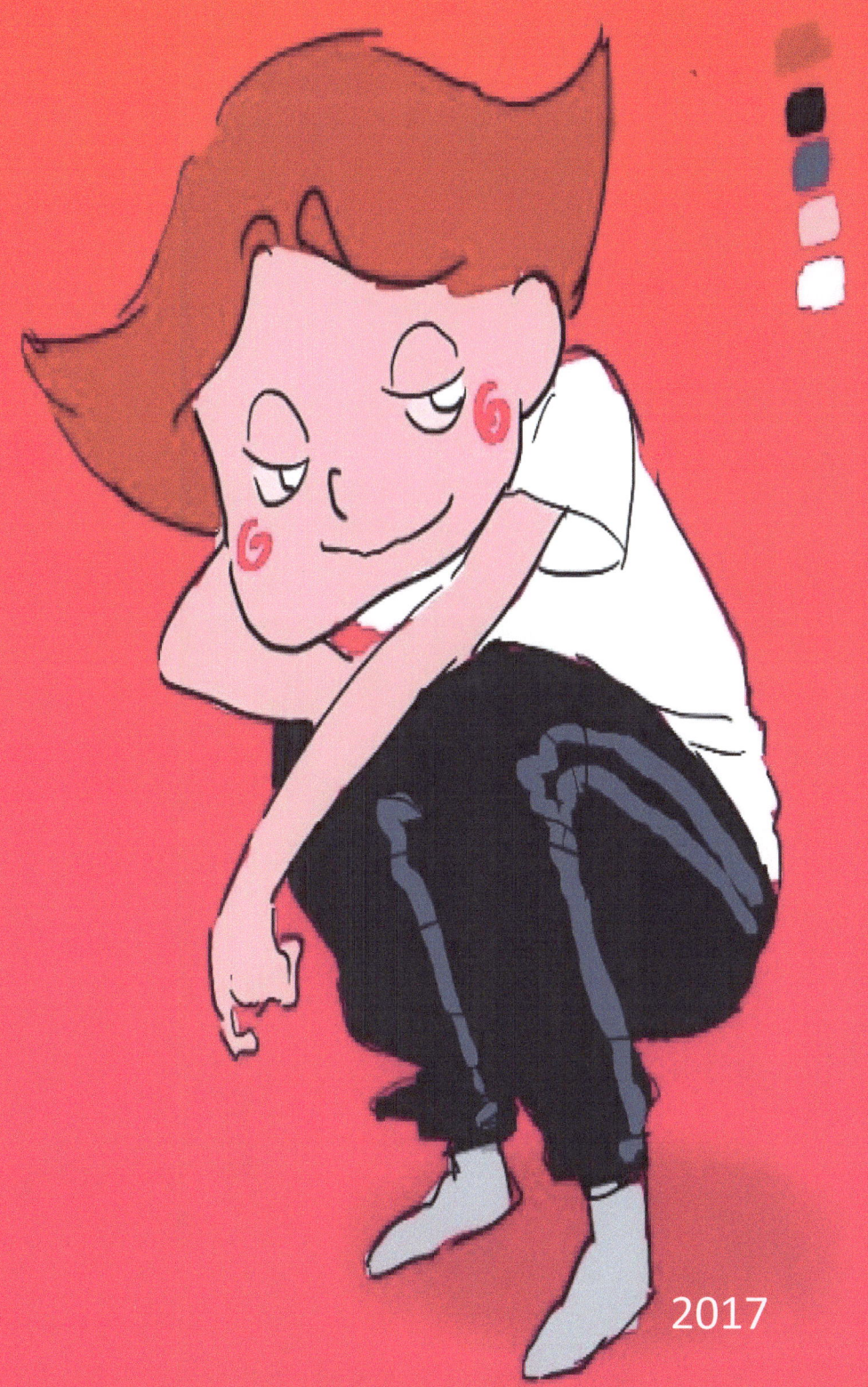

2017

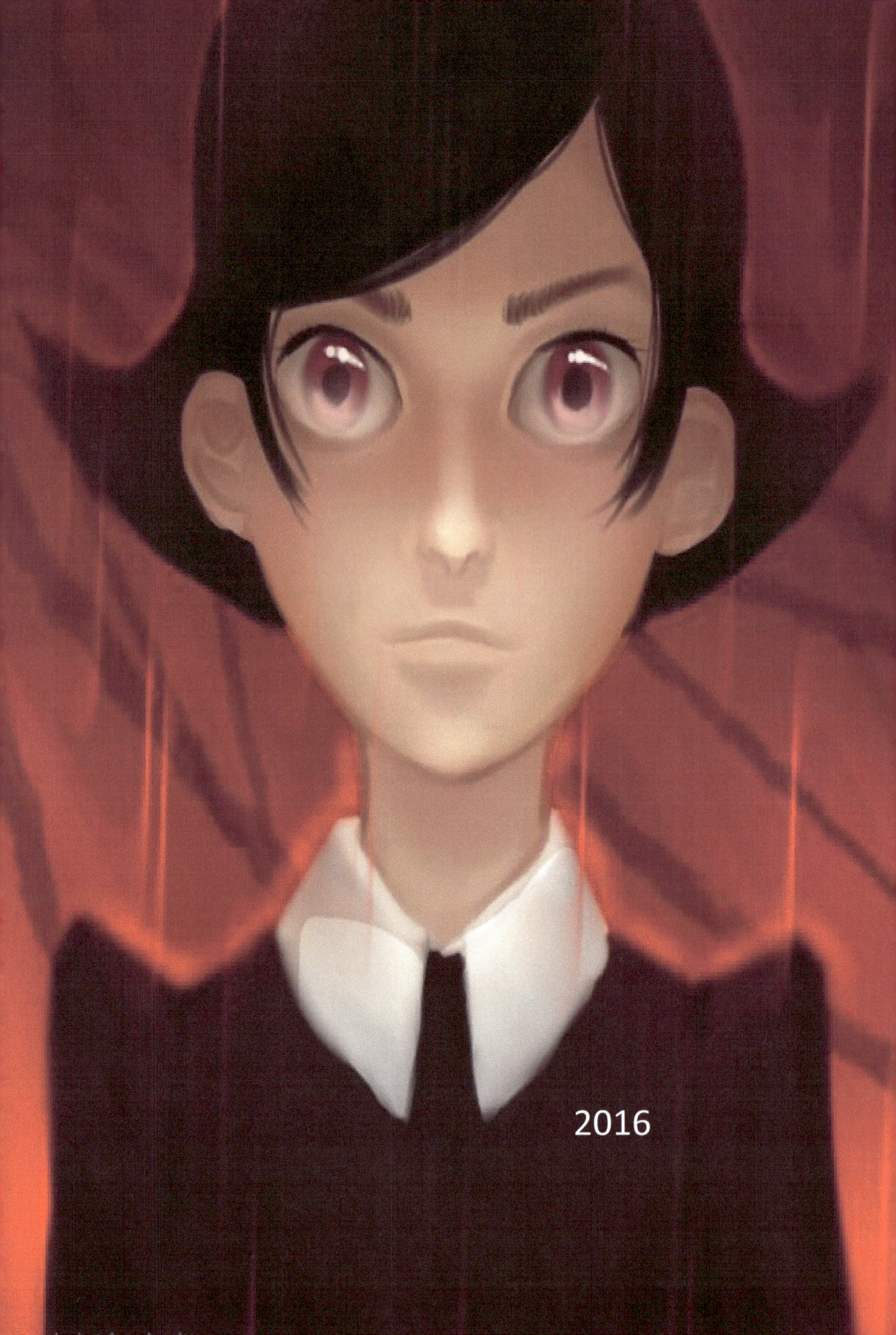

2016

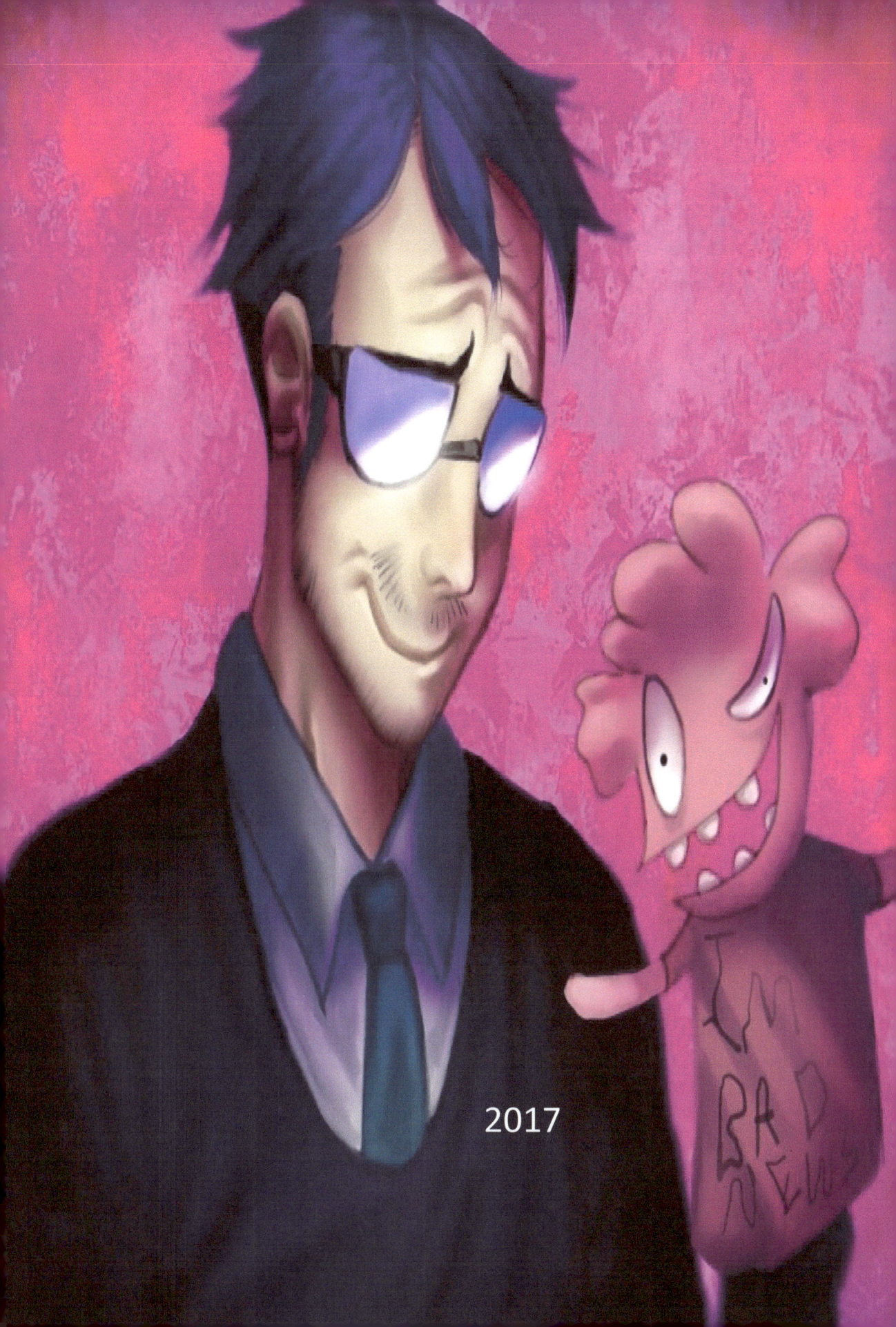

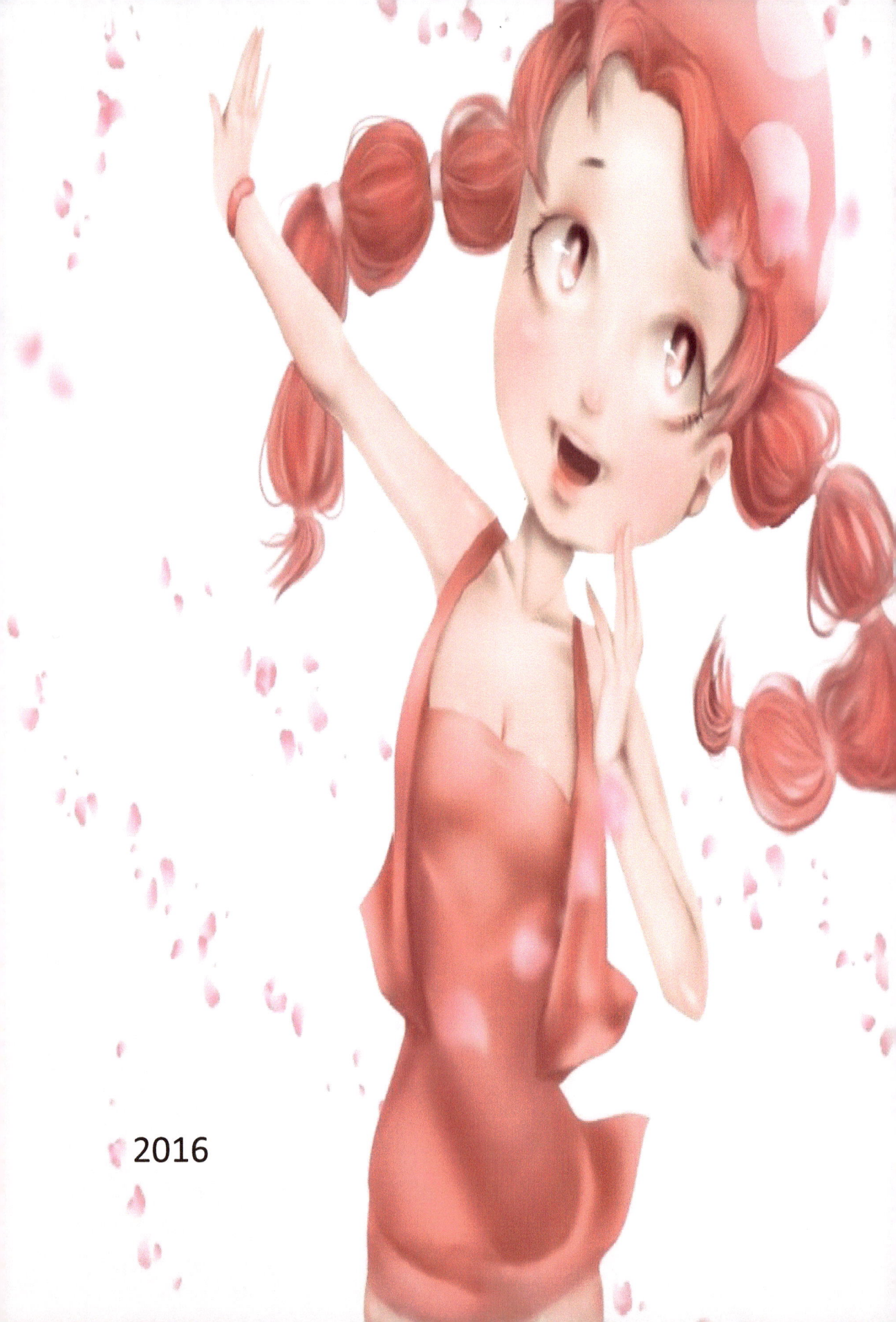

2016

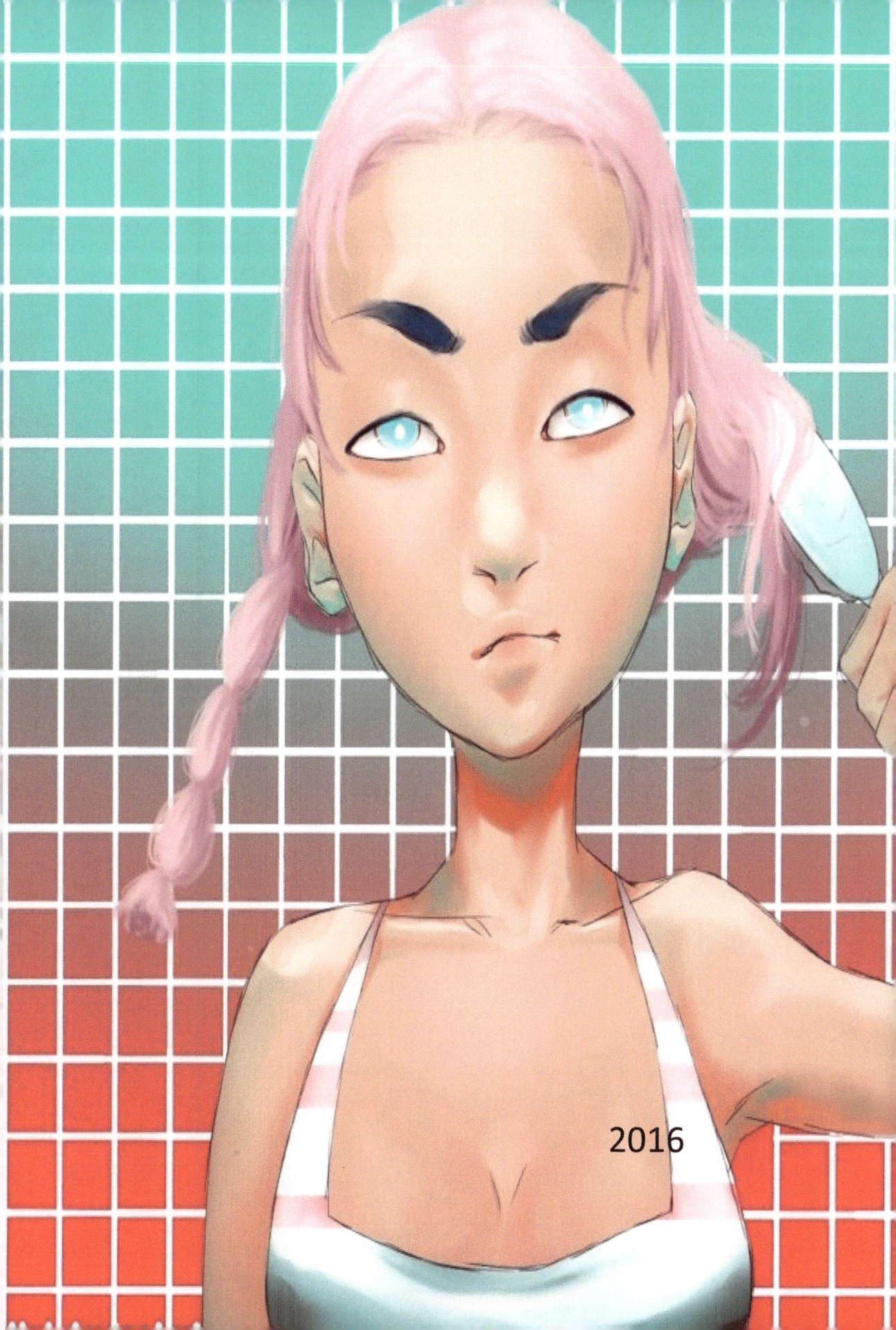

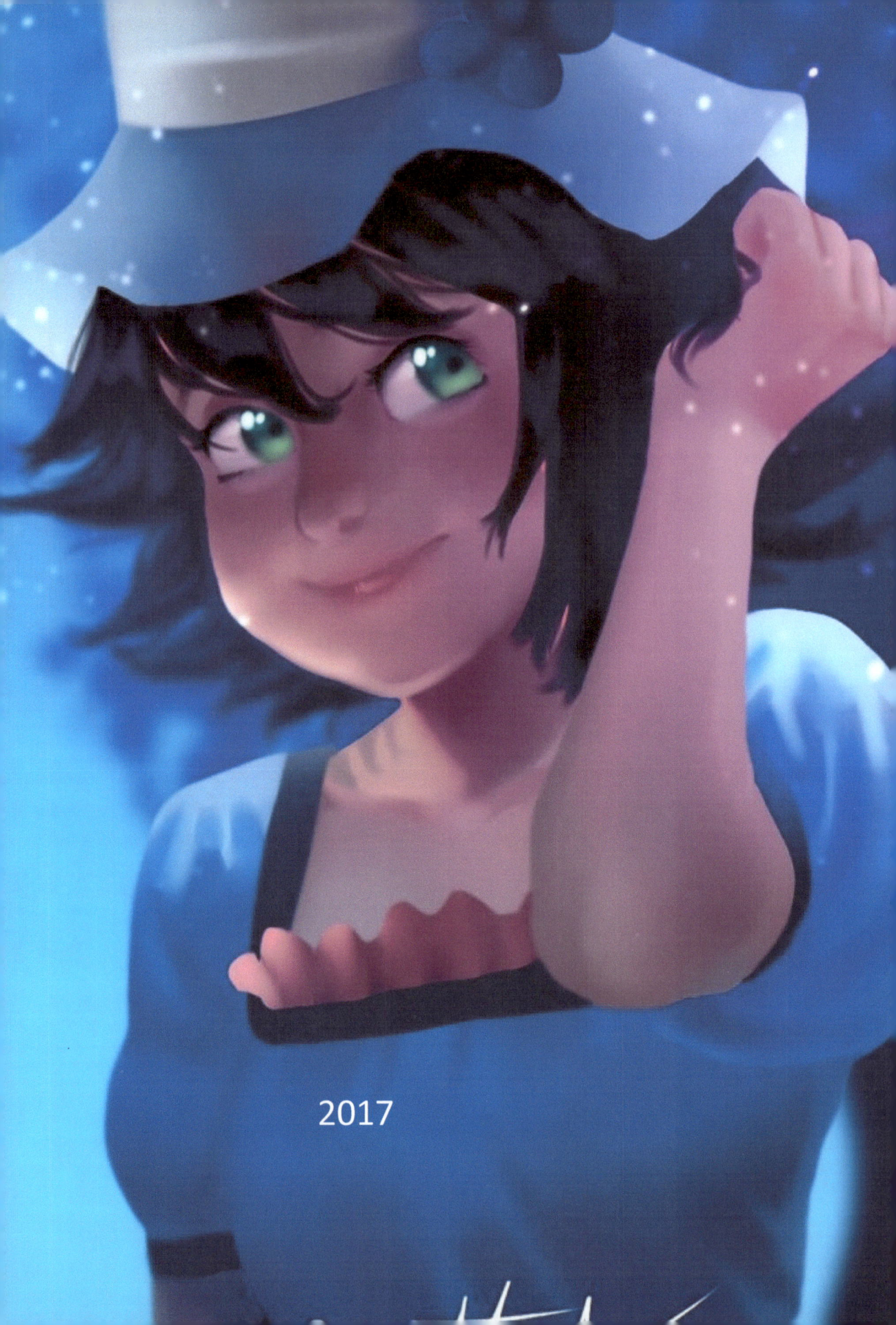

2017

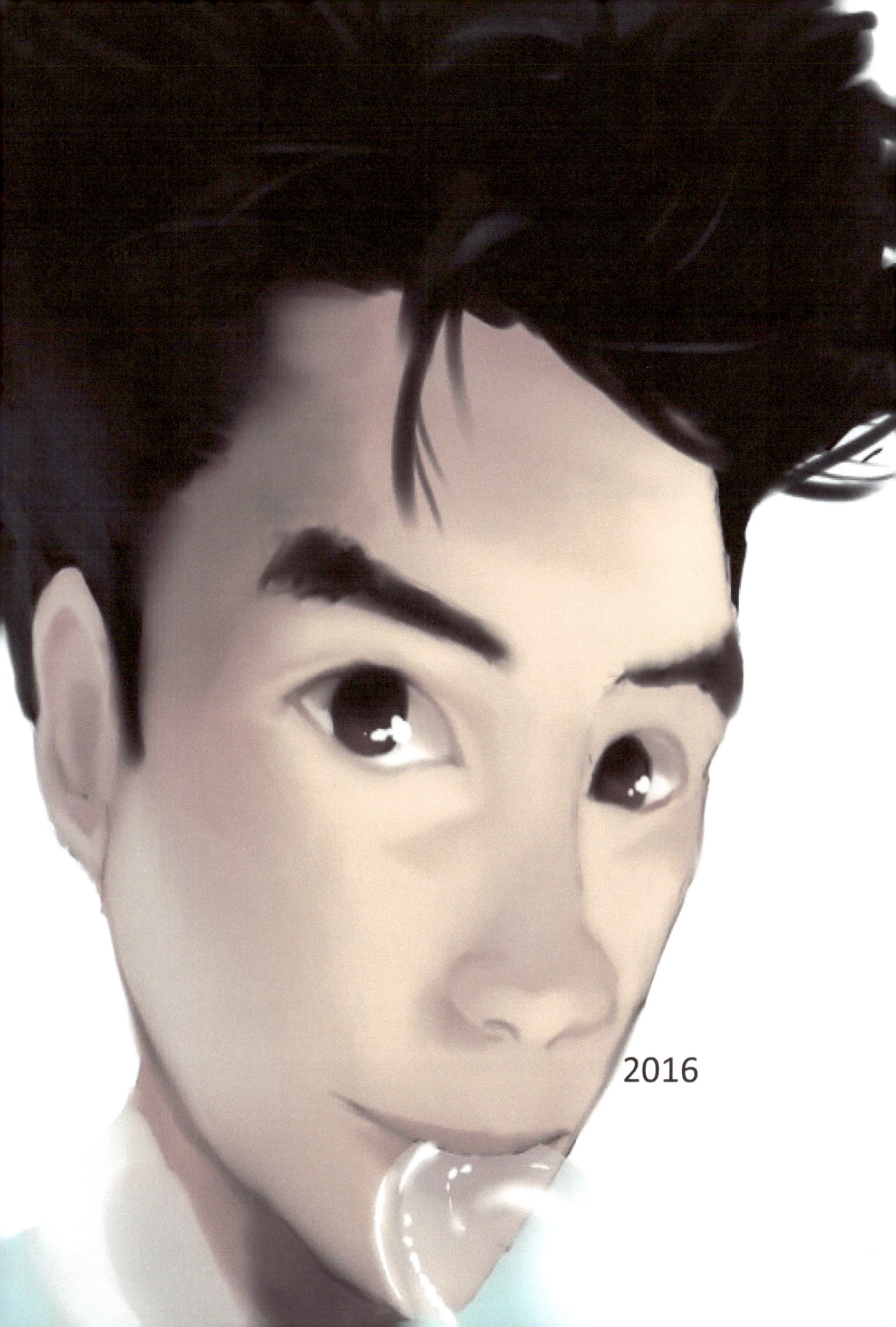

2016

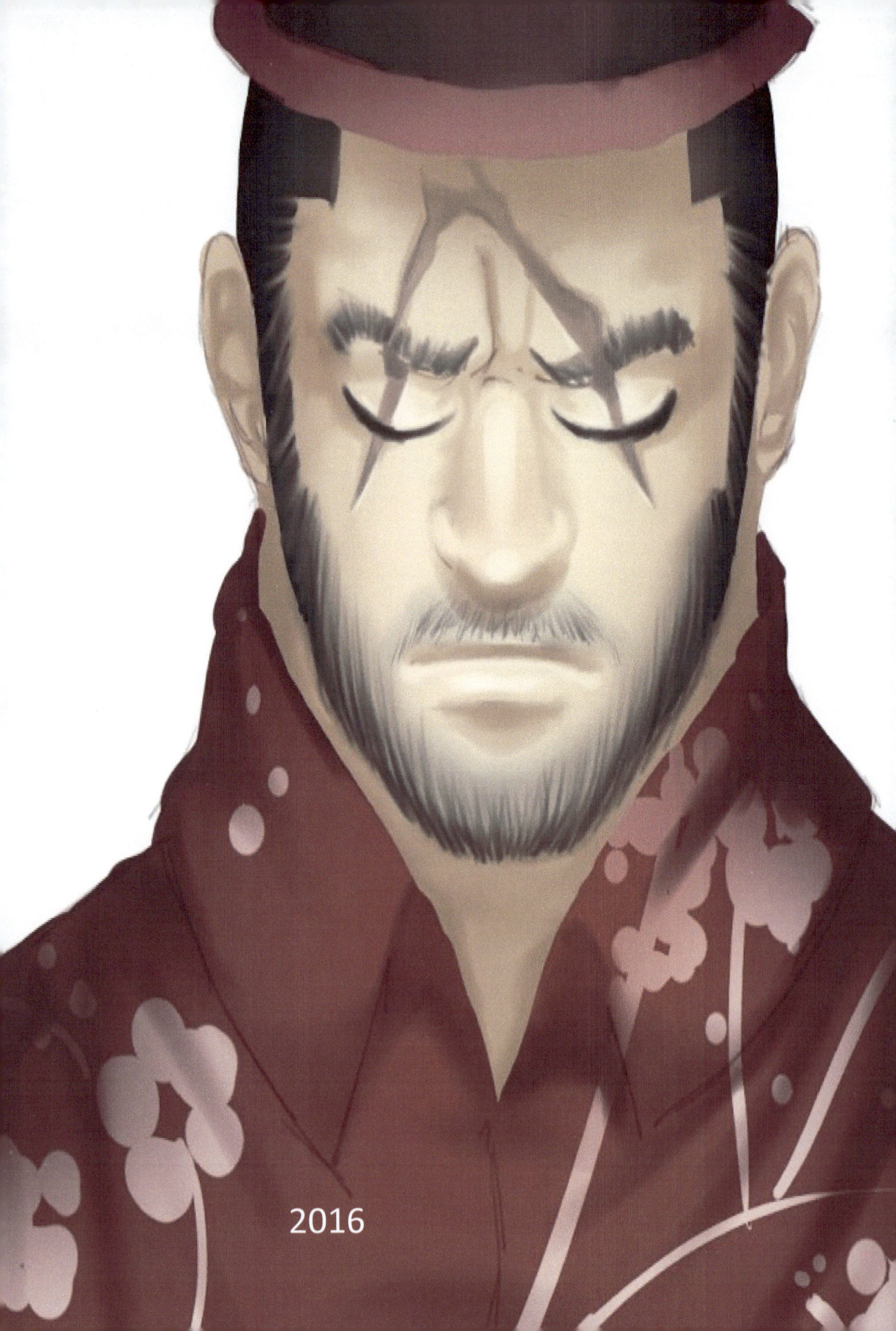

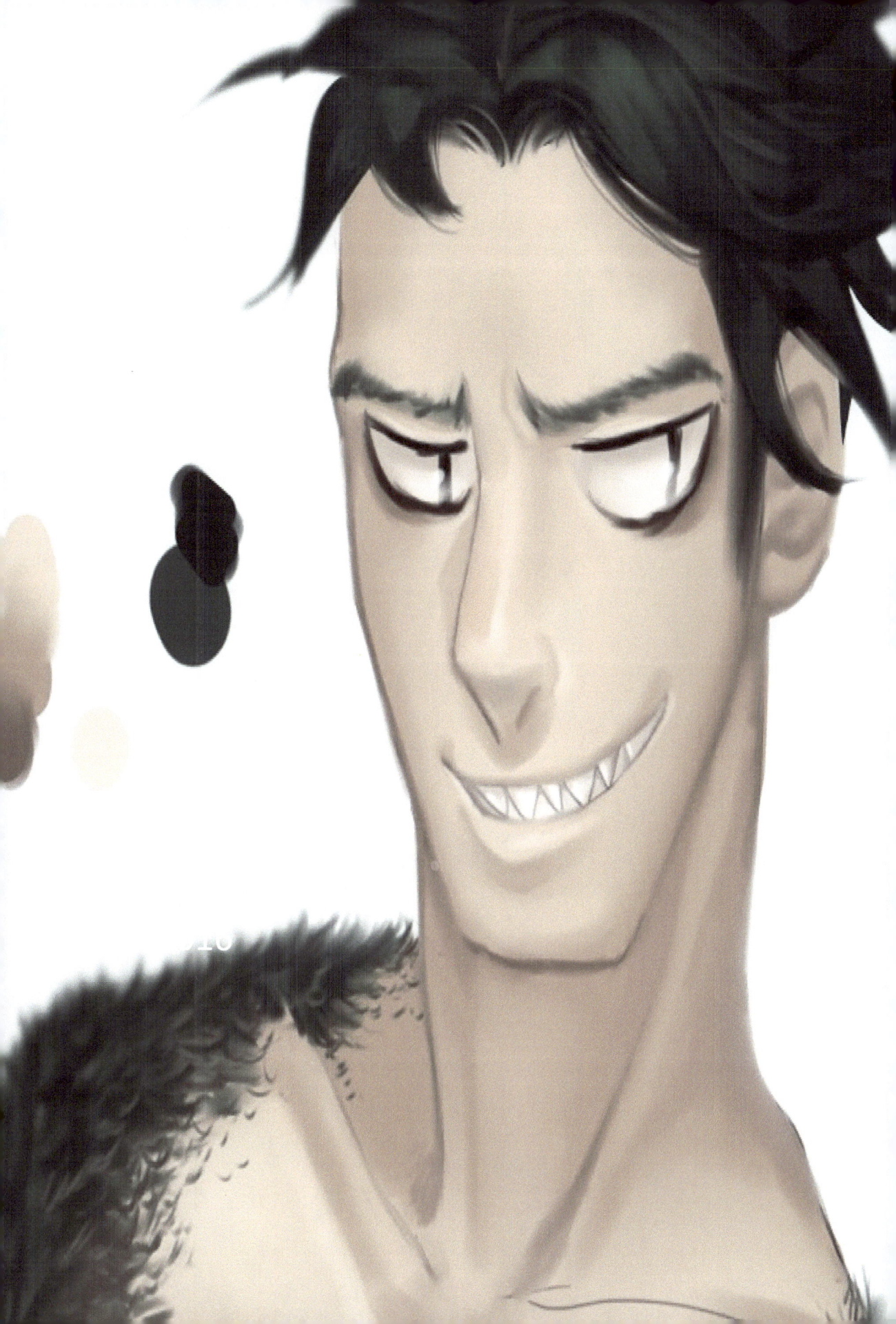

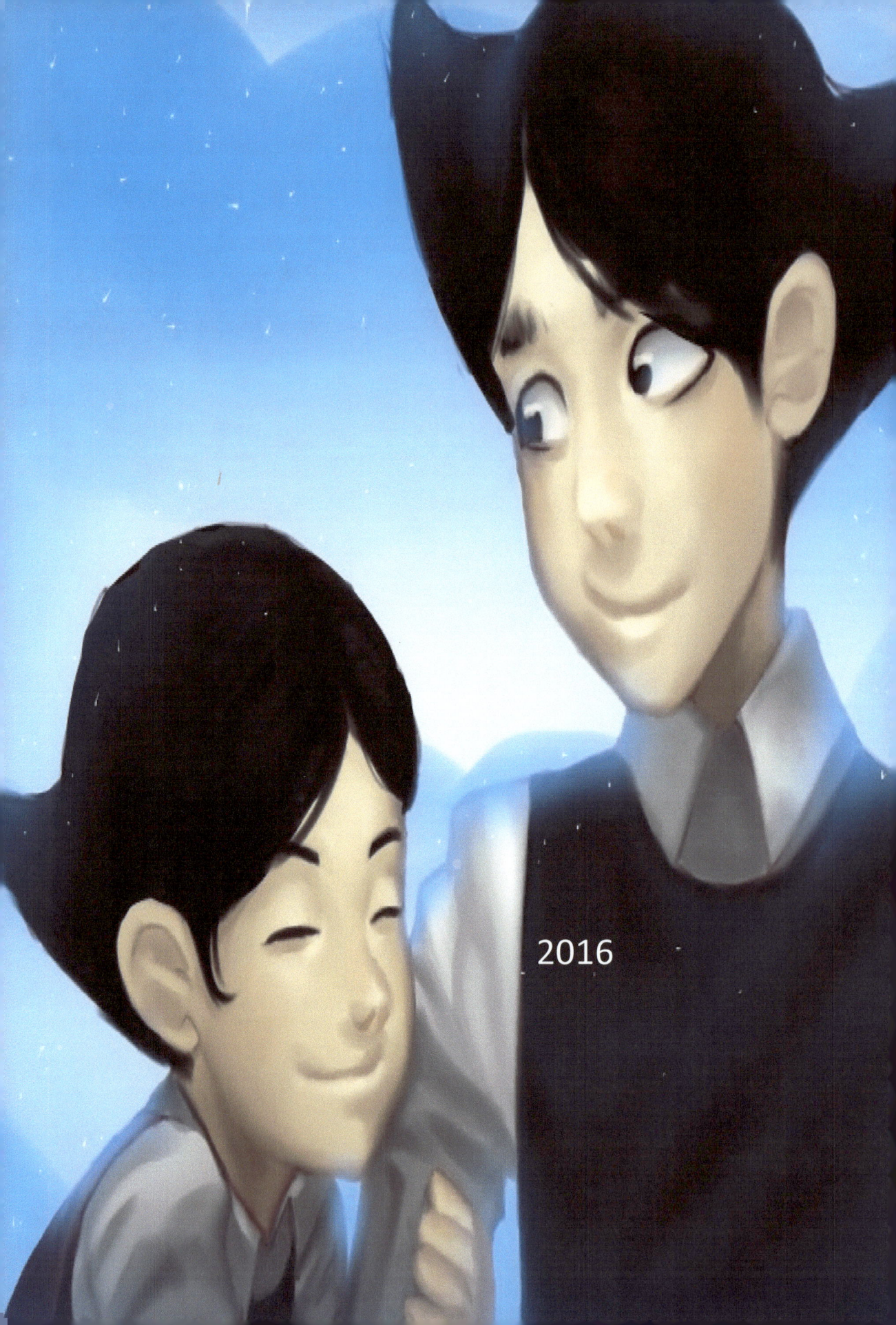

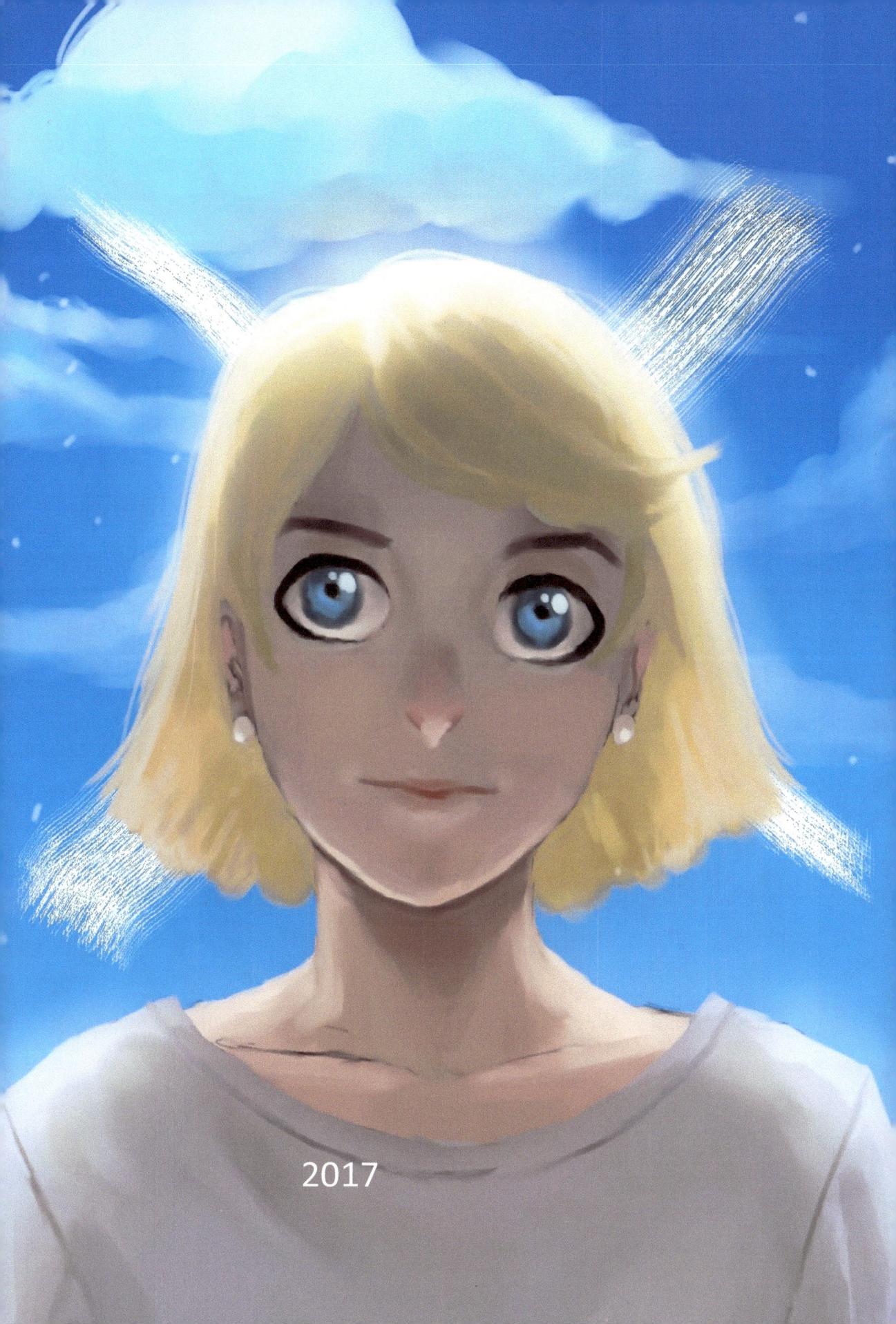
2017

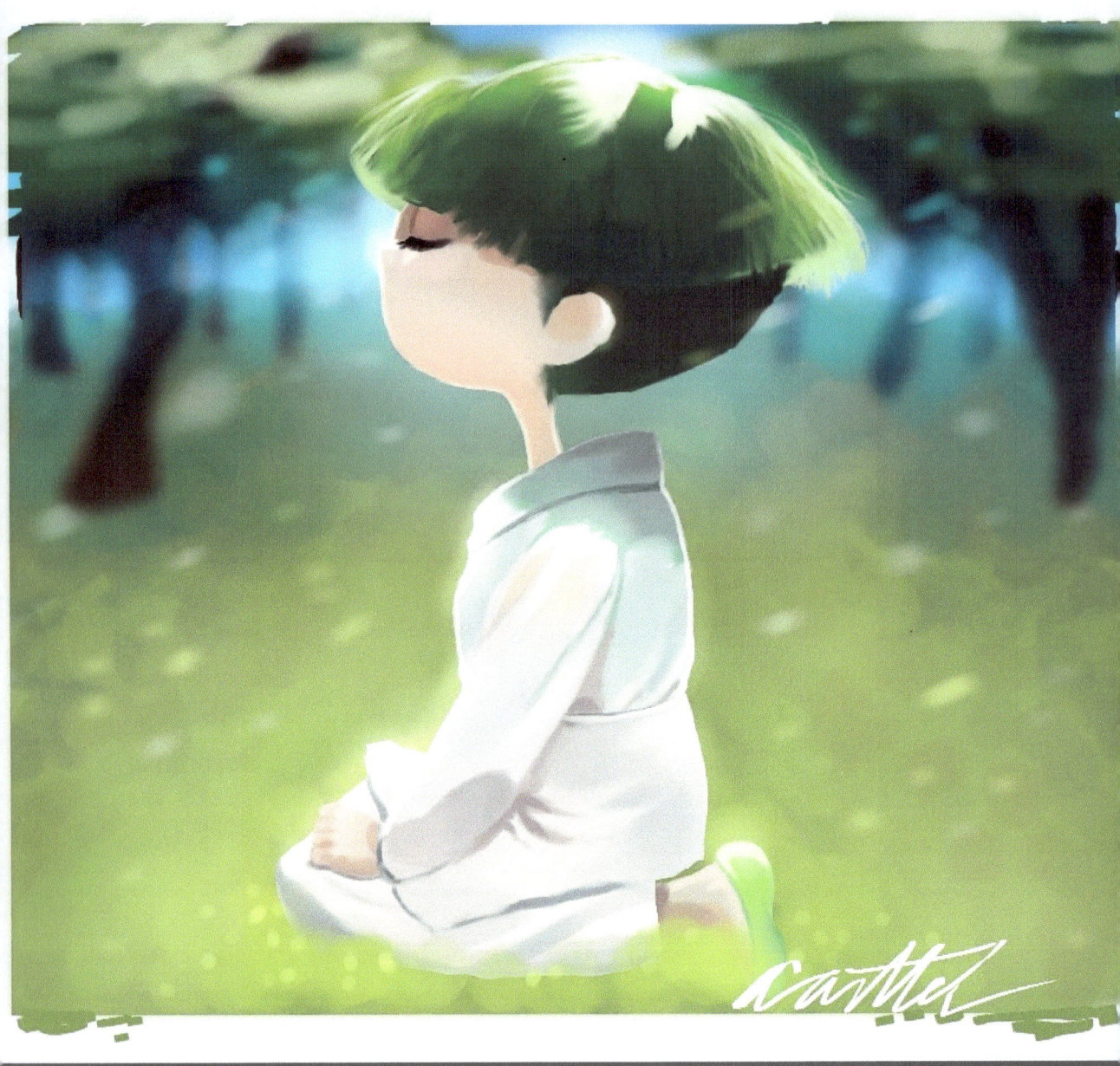

2017

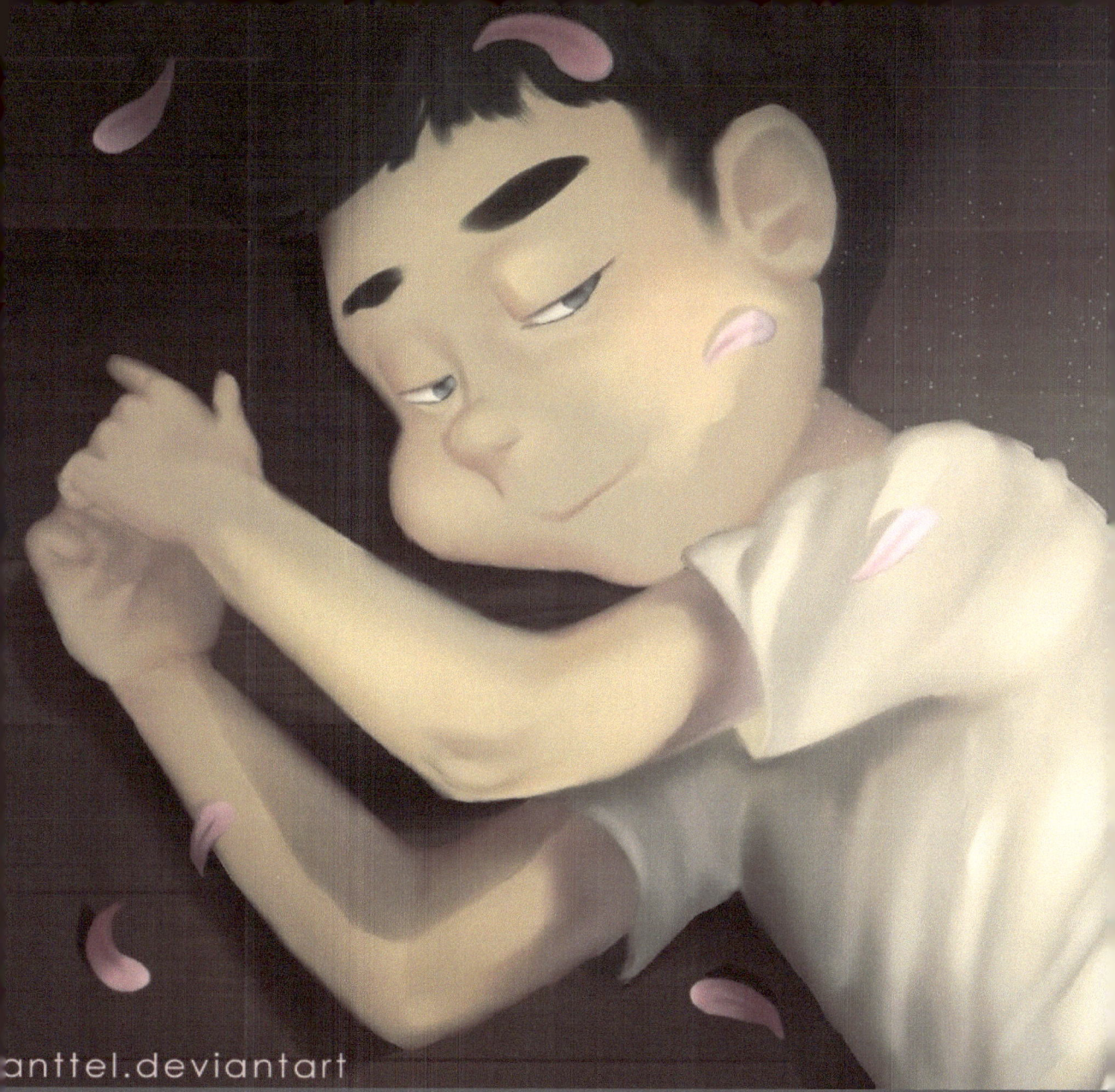

2016

The same person just genderbended!

Instagram sketches

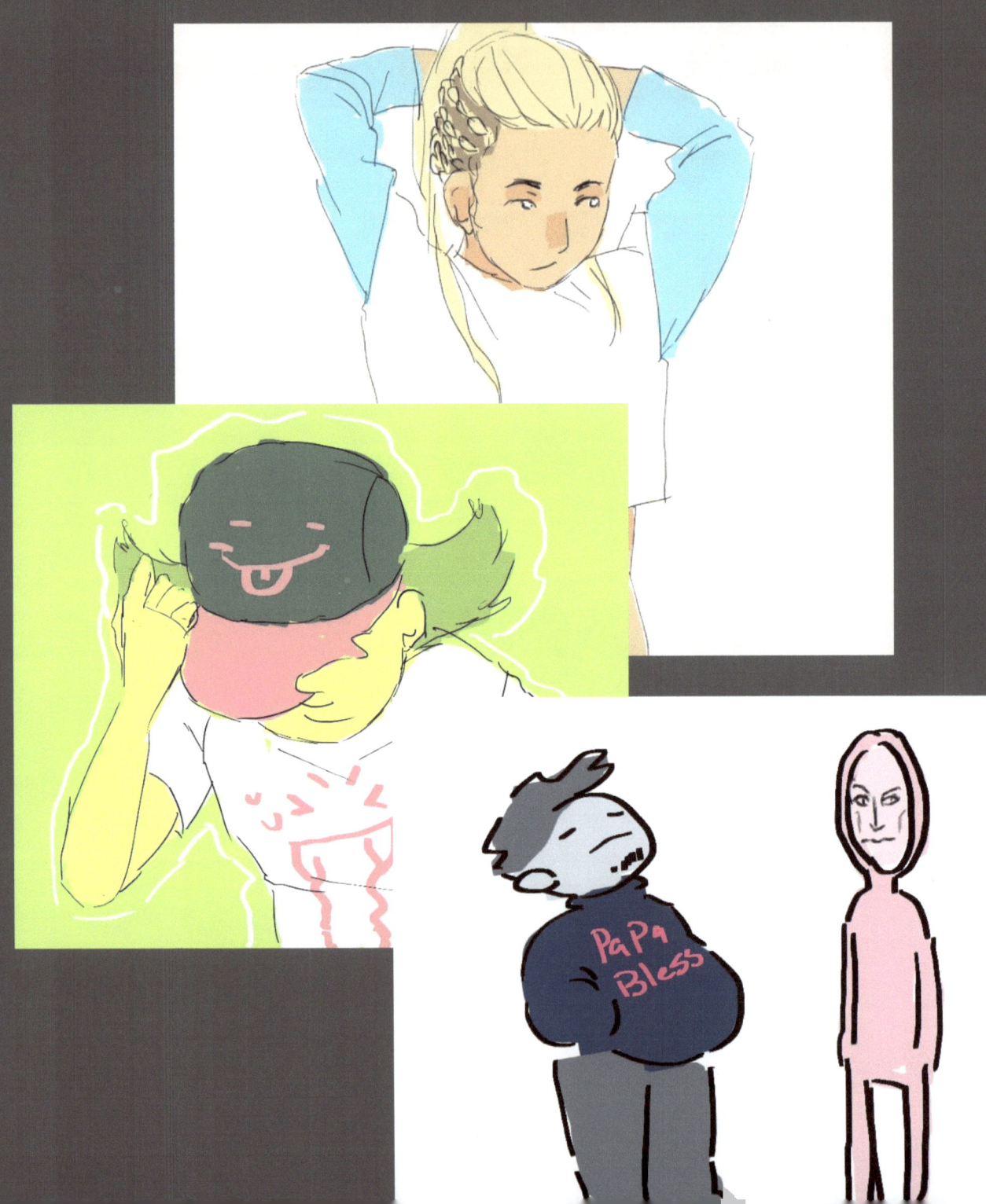

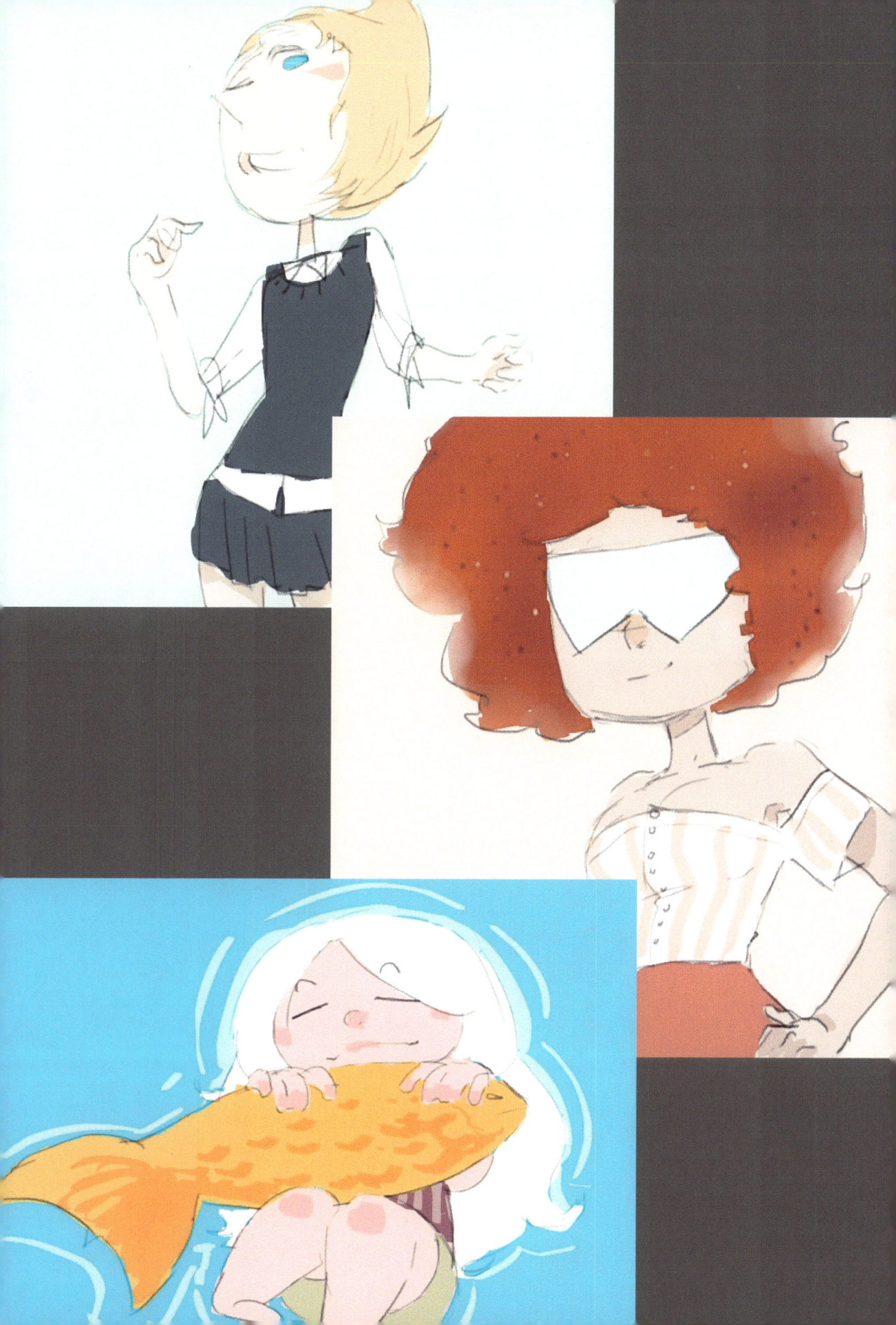

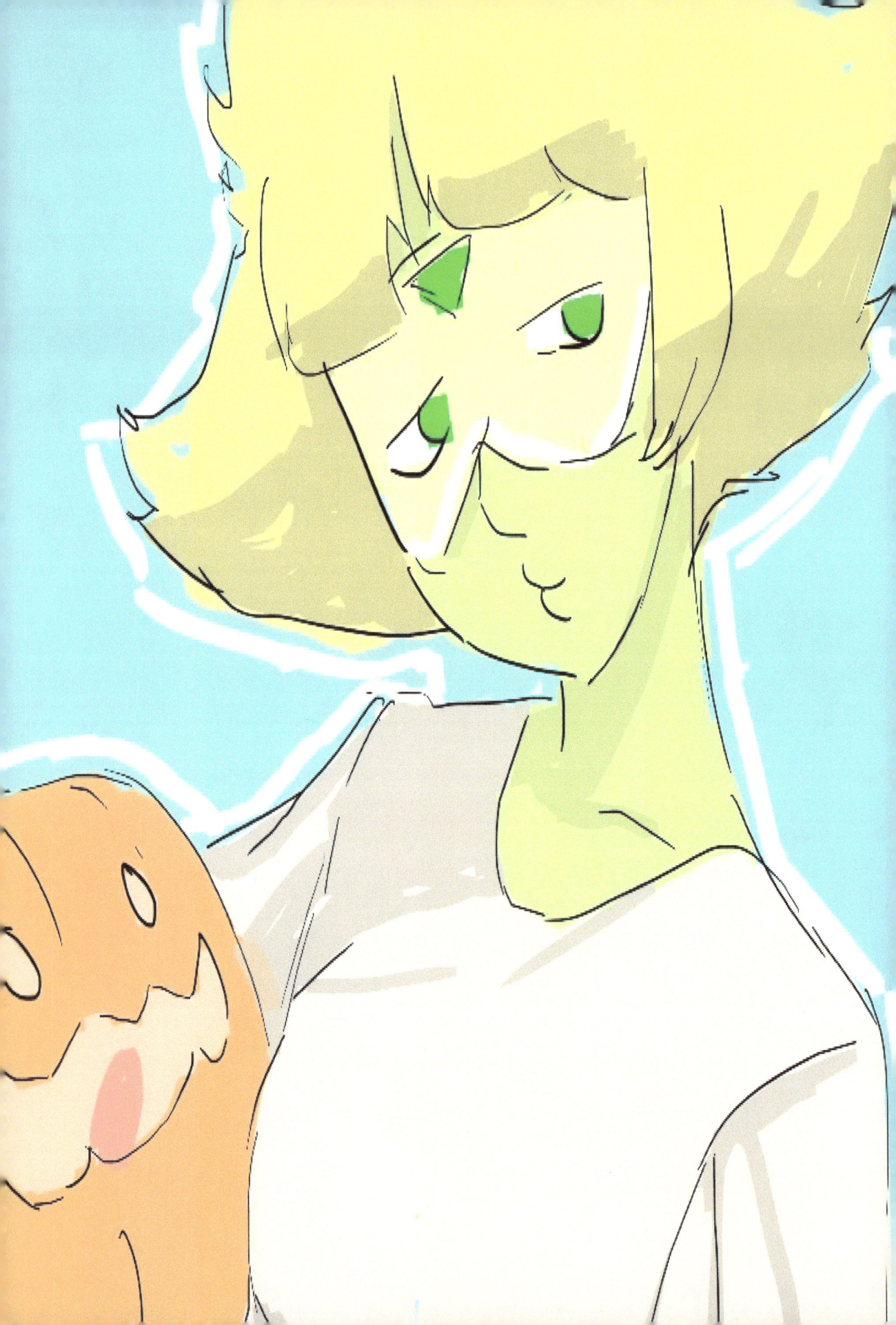

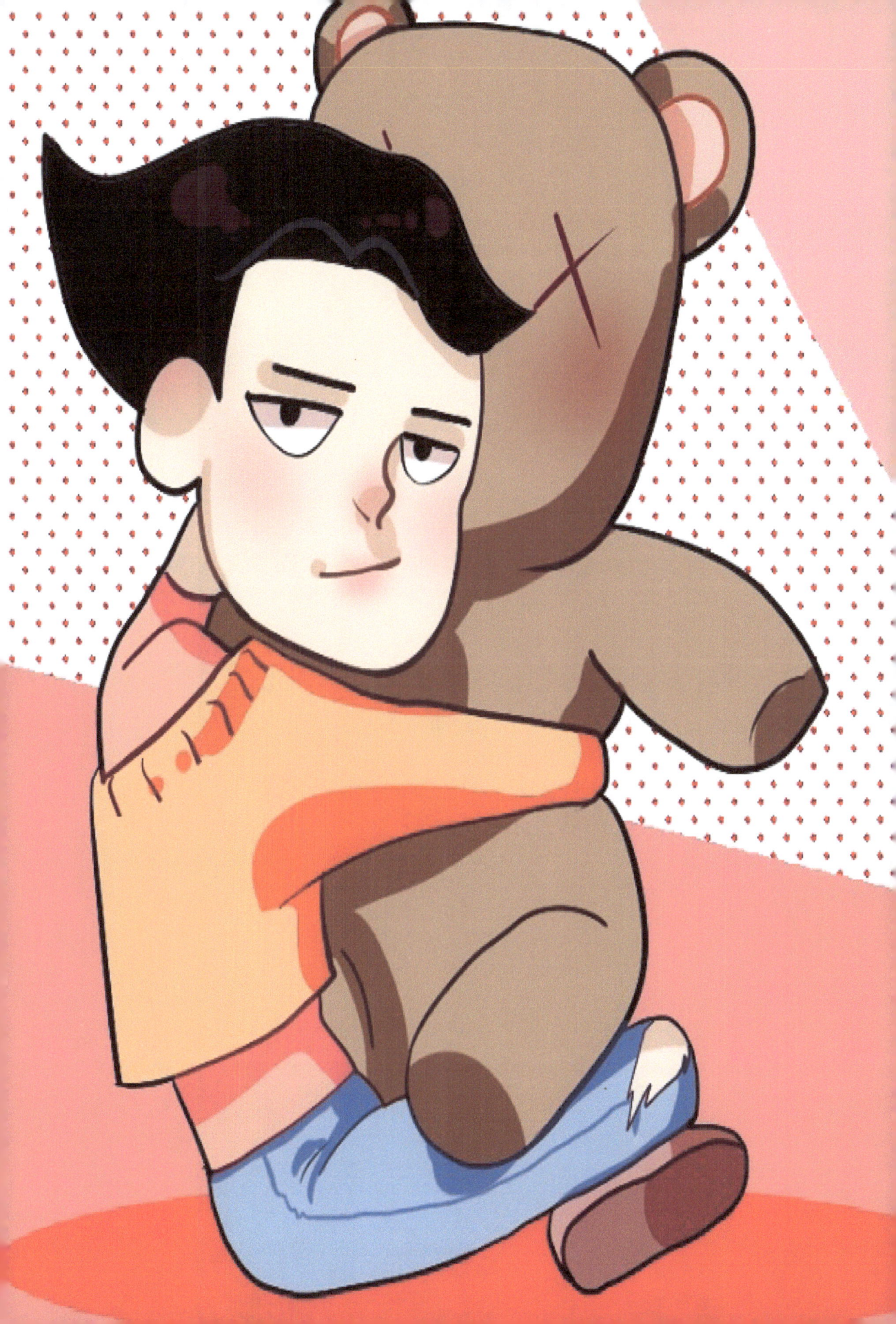

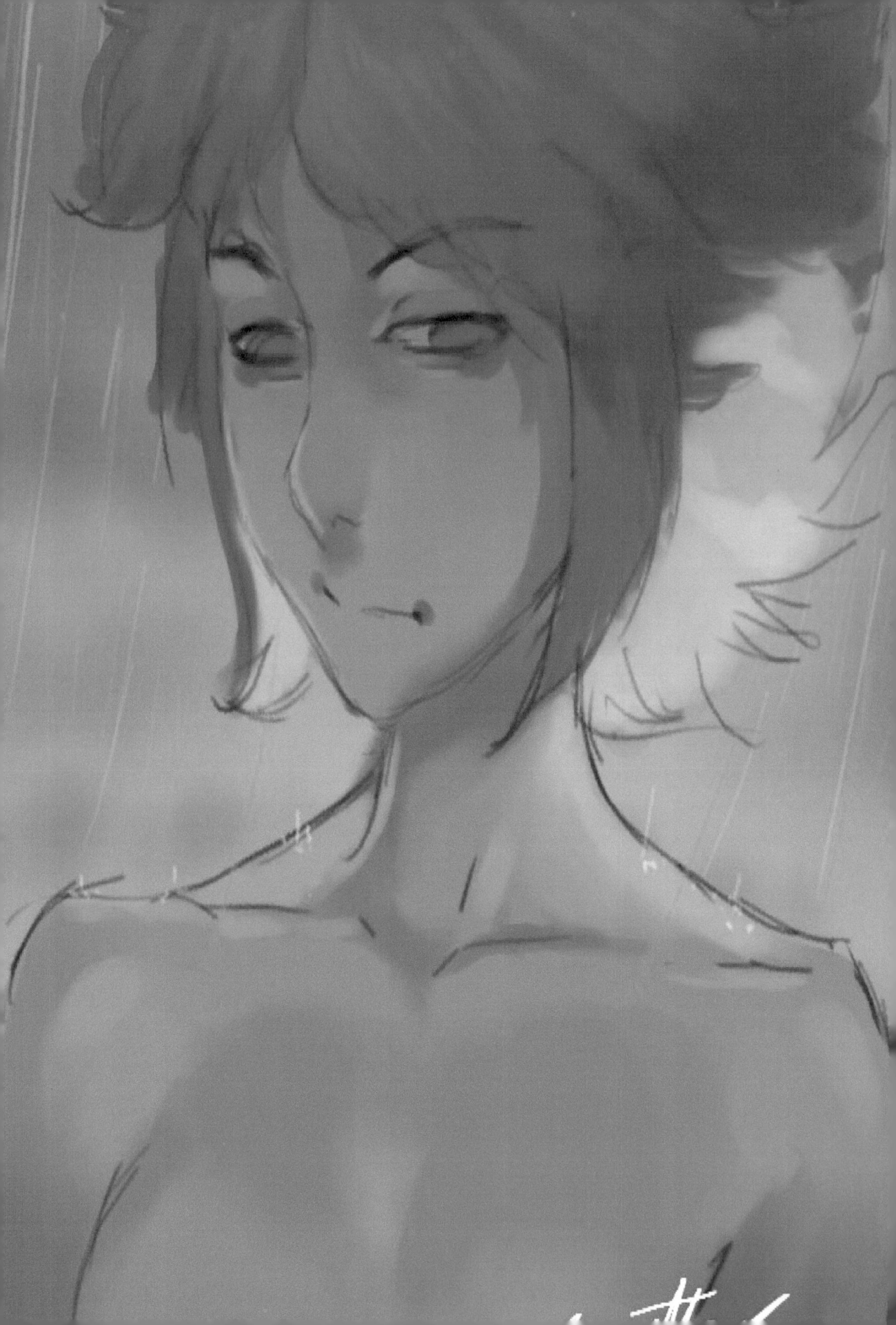

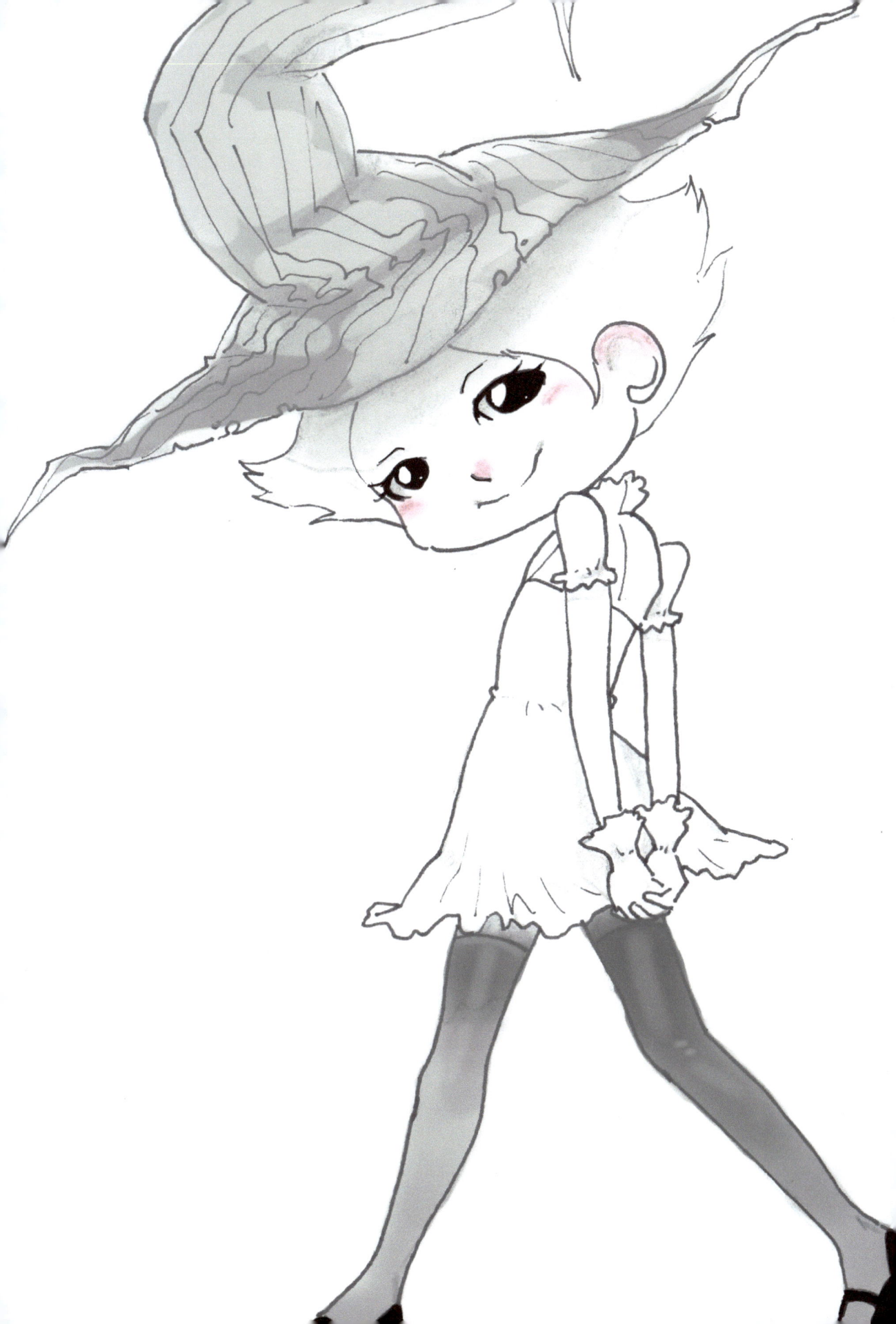

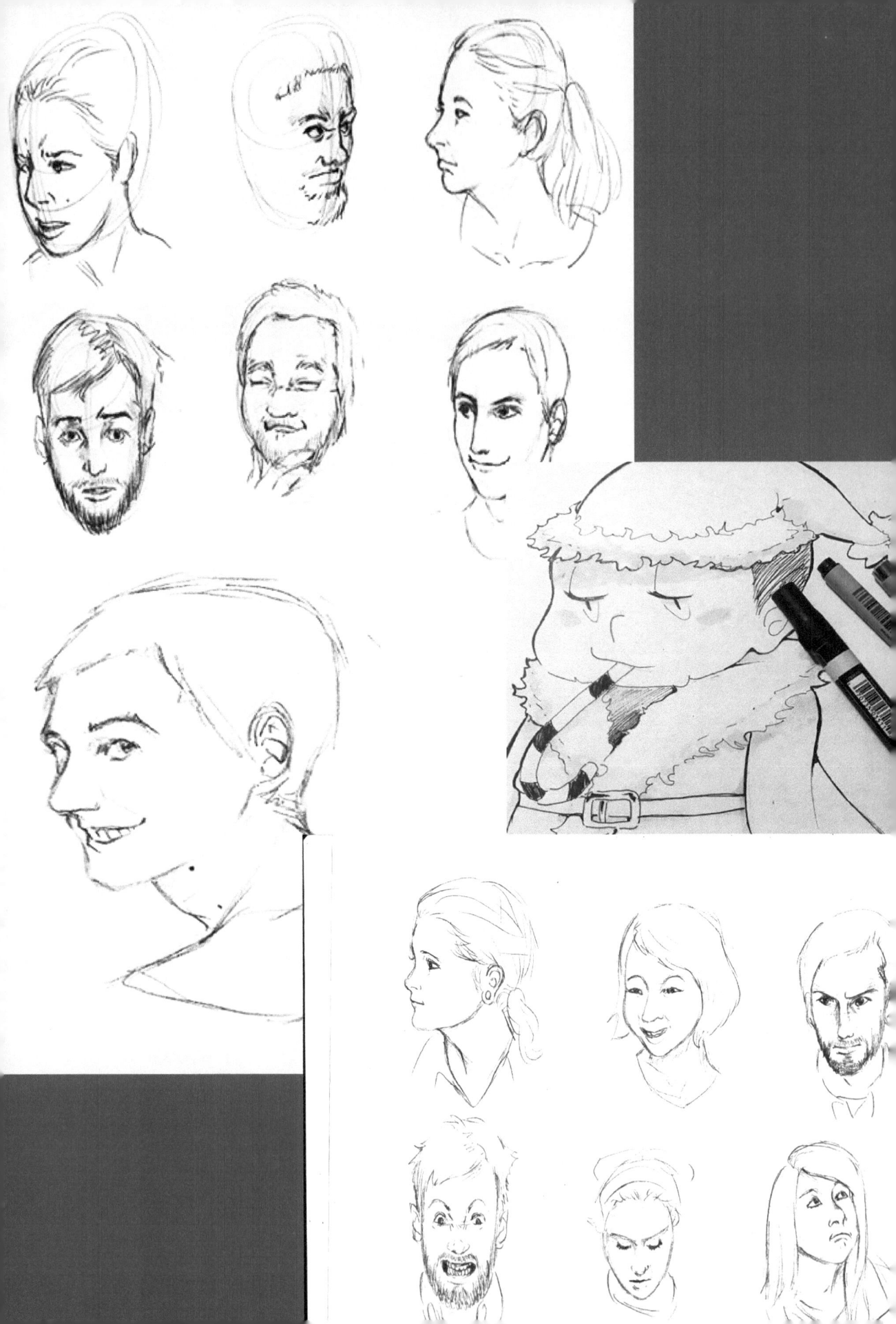

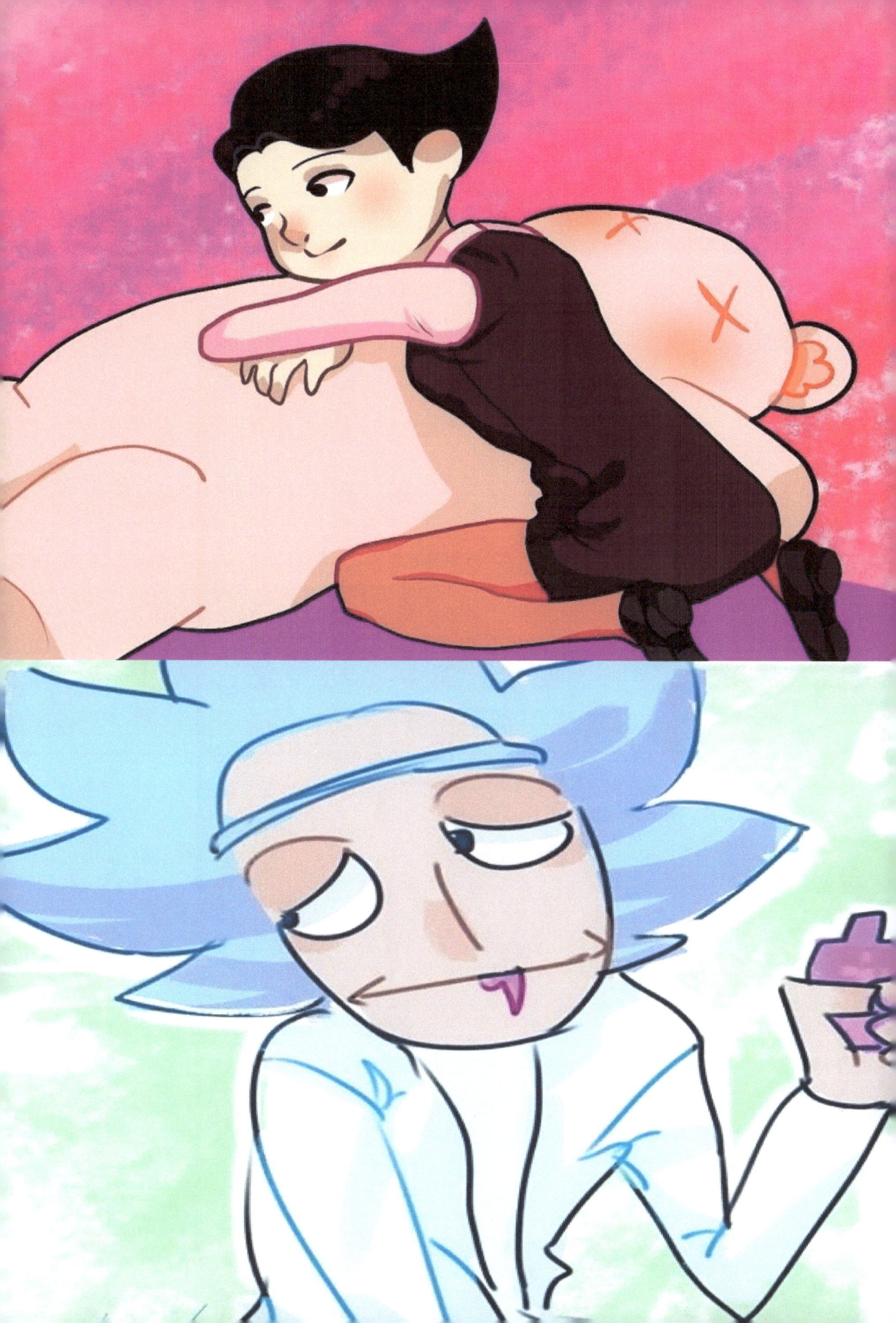

Character design

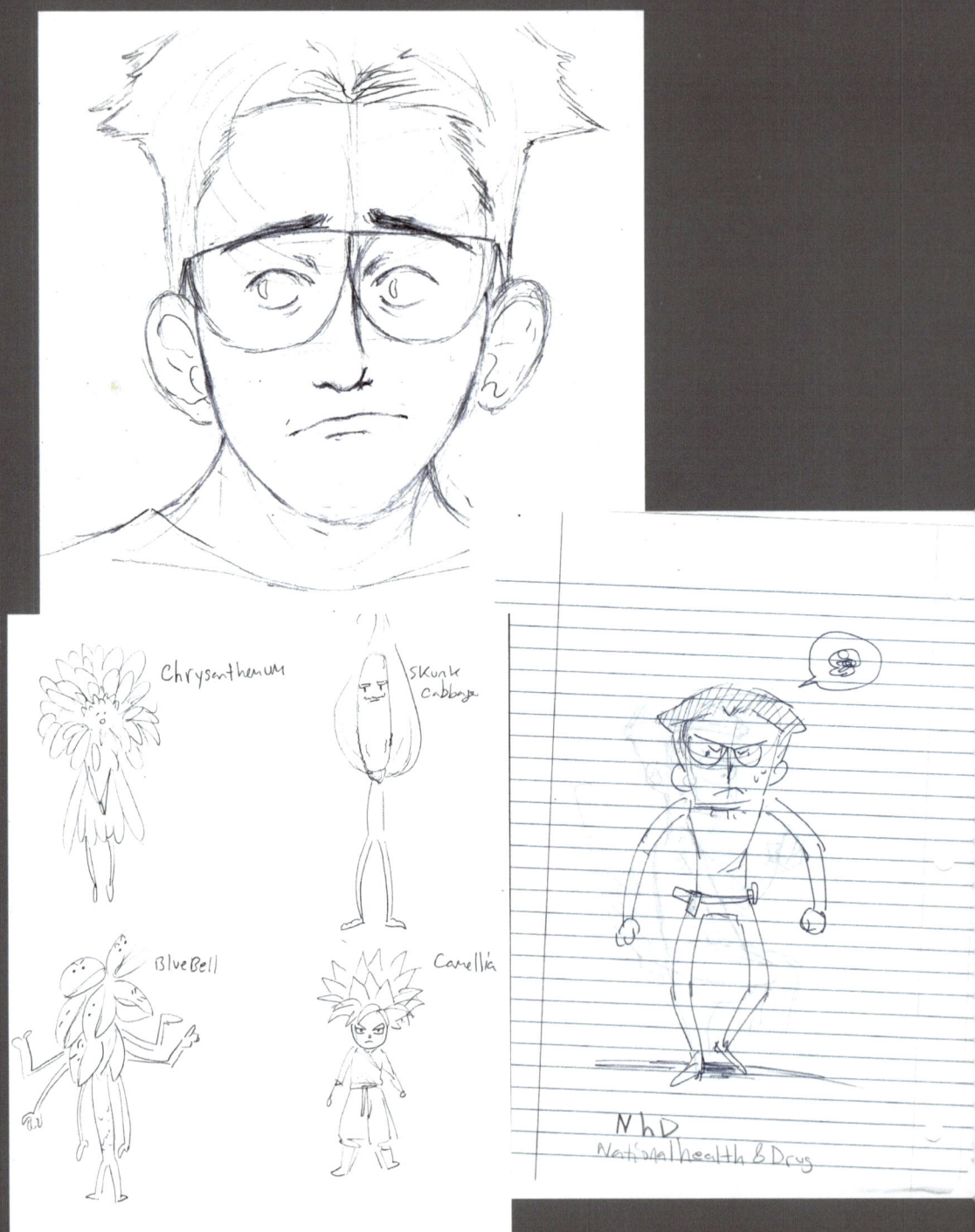

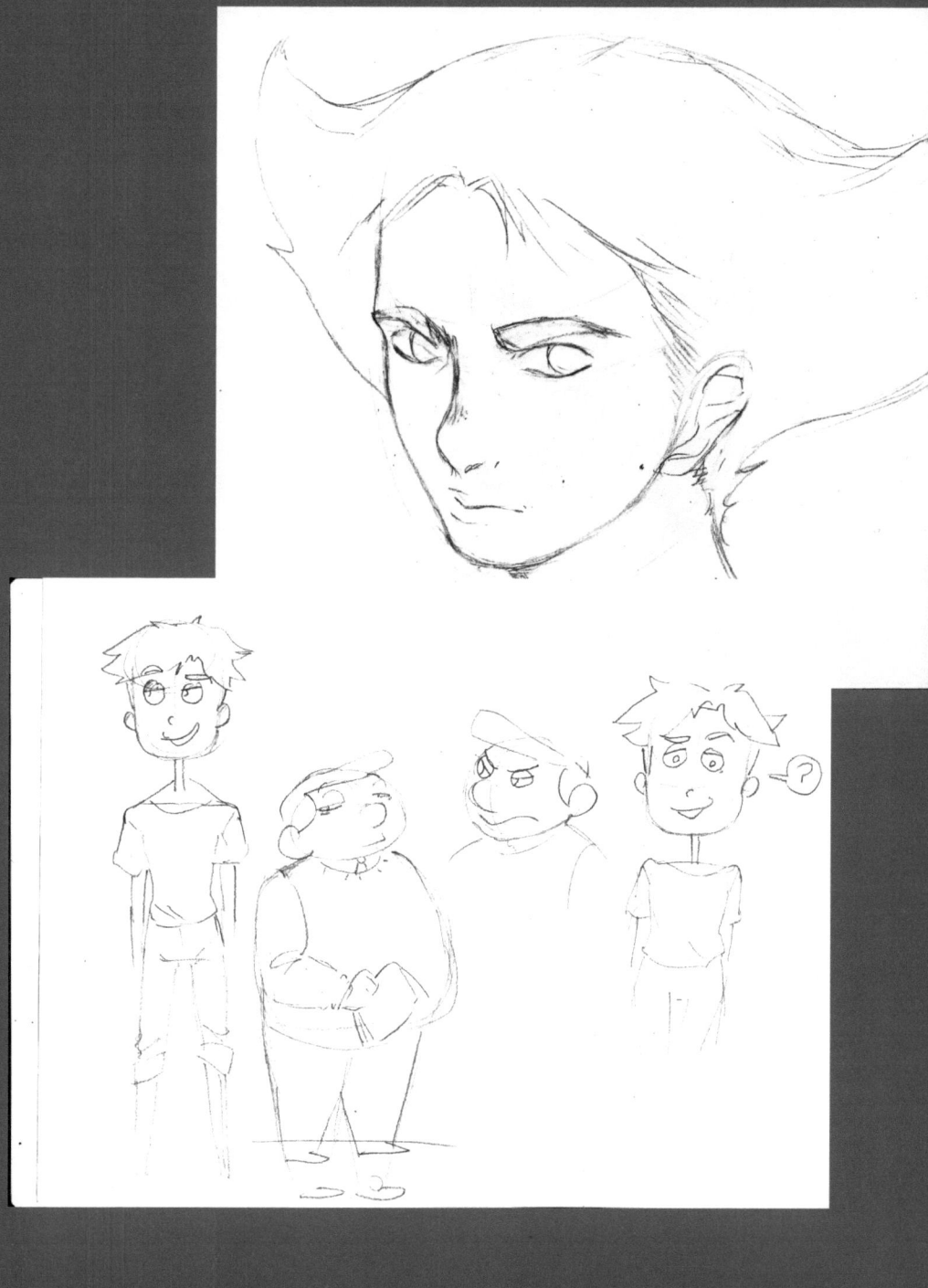